CEREBRAL PALSY

CEREBRAL PALSY

Ruth Bjorklund

mc **Marshall Cavendish**
Benchmark
New York

For Lily

With thanks to Alexander H. Hoon Jr., M.D., M.P.H., Director, Phelps Center for Cerebral Palsy and Neurodevelopmental Medicine, for his expert review of the manuscript. Dr. Hoon is a research scientist at Kennedy Krieger Institute and an Associate Professor of Pediatrics at the Johns Hopkins University School of Medicine, Baltimore, Maryland.

Marshall Cavendish Benchmark
99 White Plains road
Tarrytown, New York 10591-9001
www.marshallcavendish.us

This book is not intended for use as a substitute for advice, consultation, or treatment by a licensed medical practitioner. The reader is advised that no action of a medical nature should be taken without consultation with a licensed medical practitioner, including action that seem to be indicated by the contents of this work, since individual circumstances vary and medical standards, knowledge, and practices change with time. The publisher, author, and medical consultants disclaim all liability and cannot be held responsible for any problems that arise from the use of this book.

Library of Congress Cataloging-in-Publication Data

Bjorklund, Ruth.
  Cerebral palsy / by Ruth Bjorklund.
      p. cm. — (Health alert)
  Summary: "Explores the history, causes, symptoms, treatments, and future of cerebral palsy"—Provided by publisher.
  Includes index.
  ISBN-13: 978-0-7614-2209-9
  ISBN-10: 0-7614-2209-9
  1. Cerebral palsy—Juvenile literature. I. Title. II. Series: Health alert (New York, N.Y.)

  RC388.B56 2007
  616.8'36—dc22
                                                    2006015818

Front cover: Neuron
Title page: Section of cerebellum
Contents page: Brain anatomy
Photo Research by Candlepants Incorporated
Cover Photo: James Cavallini/Photo Researchers Inc.
The photographs in this book are used by permission and through the courtesy of: *Photo Researchers Inc.*: Anatomical Travelogue/SPL, 3, 14,15 16; Bill Andrews & Associates, Custom Medical Stock/SPL, 5, 11; Christian Darkin, 13; Shelia Terry, 17; AJPhoto, 19; AKG, 28; Malcolm Fielding, The BOC Group PLC, 37; Richard T. Nowitz, 45; Phanie, 46; Lawrence Migdale, SPL, 53. *Corbis:* Royalty Free, 20; Tom Stewart, 40. *The Image Works:* Bob Daemmrich, 12, 22, 25, 35; Ellen Sewnisi, 32; Mitch Wojnarowicz, 39. *Getty Images:* Paul J. Richards/AFP, 24; TimeLife Pictures, 29, 30; George Diebold Photography, 34; Medioimages, 42; Amos Morgan, 43; 51. *Barts and The London NHS Trust/ The Royal London Hospital Archives:* 27. PhotoTakeUSA.com: David M. Grossman, 41; Richard T. Nowitz, 48.

Printed in China
6 5 4 3 2 1

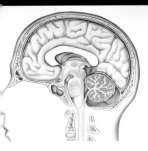

CONTENTS

WHAT IS IT LIKE TO HAVE CEREBRAL PALSY?

Five years ago, Katie first met Caroline at a horseback riding class. Caroline was having her first lesson, but Katie was not. She was seven and had already been riding for a year. Just the summer before, she had won the stable's "Best New Rider" ribbon. Katie cheered on Caroline, another seven-year-old.

There was cheering outside the riding ring, too. Both girls' parents looked on proudly as the riding instructor led their daughters through the lesson. This was a day neither set of parents had expected to see years before. Years ago they learned their babies had been born with a condition called **cerebral palsy.** At that time, they could not imagine how much their girls would accomplish in the years ahead.

Doctors had told Katie's parents that their daughter's brain had been injured at birth. Her physical development would make it difficult for her to do many things other children could do. Yet there Katie was, up in the saddle, and riding her horse around the ring.

Right after Caroline's birth, her doctors said that medical tests showed her brain had been injured even before her birth. The doctors could not say exactly what Caroline would be able or unable to do when she got older. But they believed her physical problems would make moving, walking, and running difficult. In fact, she had been using a wheelchair for several years.

All these physical activities did turn out to be difficult for both girls. But the challenges did not stop them from participating in all kinds of activities. They not only learned to ride horses, both girls swam on a special team and participated in sports. They played other games with children who also had physical challenges and some who did not.

Today, Katie and Caroline are in the same middle school classroom. A van picks up Katie outside her door then travels across town to pick up six other **special education** students, including Caroline. When they get to Caroline's house, the rear door of the bus opens, and a loud beep alerts others that the driver is lowering a ramp for Caroline's electric wheelchair.

Katie and Caroline begin their mornings in a special education classroom with other students who have physical and learning **disabilities,** or challenges. Two teachers and four helpers, called **para-educators,** help the students get ready for the day by going over their schedules and homework. Along with nondisabled students, Katie goes to regular classes for science, math, social studies, and language arts with her para-educator. One period a day, Katie works on homework and computer skills in the special **resource room.** That is when she and Caroline see each other during the school day. Several times a week, **physical therapists** and **occupational therapists** visit the resource room. They help Katie and Caroline and others to develop fine-motor skills, such as writing or cutting with scissors and using a computer keyboard. A yoga teacher works with the girls to develop their large motor skills with stretching exercises.

Caroline takes computer and art classes with nondisabled students. In the computer classroom, Caroline uses an "Intellikey" keyboard, which can be programmed to make typing easier for her. In the self-contained special education classroom, Caroline, who is both physically and mentally disabled, gets extra time and attention to help her read, write, and learn basic math, such as using money. A speech and language therapist works with Caroline to help her pronounce words more clearly. Like many twelve-year-olds, Caroline loves talking on the phone. Her speech therapist uses phone conversation to help Caroline improve her communication skills.

Both Katie and Caroline love school, their teachers, yoga class, and computers. After school, they attend school dances, band concerts, and plays. Their lives at home are filled with family, friends, and a lot of pets they love and care for. Both girls get to the beach in summer, attend summer camp, and continue to ride horses whenever possible. Through the parks department in their town, Caroline and Katie take pottery, dance, cooking, and swimming lessons. Whenever the girls sign up for an activity, there are additional counselors there to help with their individual needs.

Katie and Caroline know that they will always require a little extra help and more time to do things. Katie will never drive a car. Caroline will never walk. Neither girl will be able to live completely on her own. But that does not stop both girls from trying everything they can.

"Nothing comes easy for them," says their yoga teacher. "But they are creative in adapting. They are *'differently* abled,' not *dis*abled." The ordinary tasks that are simple for most people, such as tying shoelaces, setting a table, pouring a glass of milk, or carrying a notebook, are huge physical challenges for the girls. Sometimes they each wish they could move around more easily, the way other kids their age do. But on most days, they take on every challenge with determination, plenty of humor, and patience.

[2]

WHAT IS CEREBRAL PALSY?

Cerebral palsy, often shortened to CP, is the name for a group of brain disorders that affect a person's movements. Before birth, abnormal brain development and injuries cause the majority of cerebral palsy cases. However, early childhood injuries, or very rare inherited diseases, lead to cerebral palsy in 10 percent of the children who show symptoms of CP later in childhood. CP is not an infection that someone can "catch" from someone else.

People with cerebral palsy have difficulty controlling posture, balance, and movement. Depending on the type and severity of the brain injury or abnormal development that has taken place, some people with CP may also have cognitive or intellectual delays or disabilities. That means they are slower to learn language, reading, and everyday living skills. Some also have problems with vision, hearing, or swallowing. Others may develop **seizures.** These are disruptions of electrical activity in the brain that can lead to abnormal body movements or sudden, brief periods of unconsciousness.

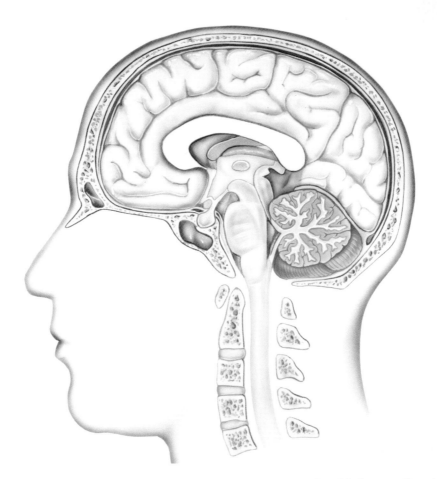

Injury to any part of the developing brain before, during, or after birth may affect how other parts of the body will work.

In the United States, approximately two to three children in a thousand have cerebral palsy. Most cases begin before birth while the **fetus** is developing. Although doctors often diagnose CP in infants soon after birth, the condition may not be obvious, or even show up, until the child is one or two years old. Head injuries, brain infections, and specific genetic diseases cause early-childhood cerebral palsy.

Cerebral palsy is a lifelong condition that can be mild to severe in degree. In some people, the problems are so mild that

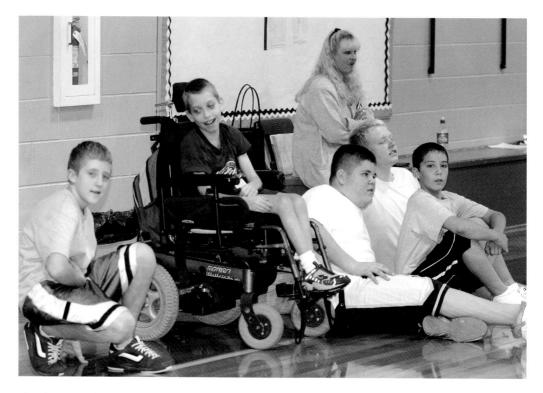

Five boys, and a wheelchair, make this flag tag team a winner in gym class.

the term cerebral palsy may or may not be used to describe them. Most children with CP do reach adulthood.

While there is no cure for cerebral palsy, there is effective treatment. Physical, occupational, and speech therapy have helped many children with cerebral palsy to live full, active lives within their families, schools, and workplaces. Special education programs in the United States have made it possible for children with cerebral palsy to attend schools with non-disabled students. Computers and other technological aids have helped children and adolescents with cerebral palsy to learn more in school and to become more active in their lives than most people thought possible years ago.

THE NERVOUS SYSTEM AND BRAIN

Cerebral palsy affects the motor centers in the brain. These motor centers control everything the body does—moving, seeing, hearing, speaking, thinking, eating, drinking, breathing, digesting food, and more.

The **nervous system** is divided into two main parts—the **central nervous system** and the **peripheral nervous system.** Both the central nervous system and the peripheral nervous system must work smoothly for involuntary and voluntary movement to occur.

The Central Nervous System

Brain cells called **neurons** and **white matter connections** in the brain and **spinal cord** make up the central nervous system. The spinal cord is a large pathway that runs the length of

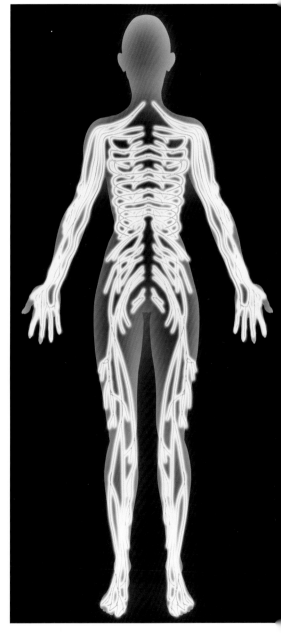

The peripheral nervous system is responsible for carrying signals about muscle movements throughout the body.

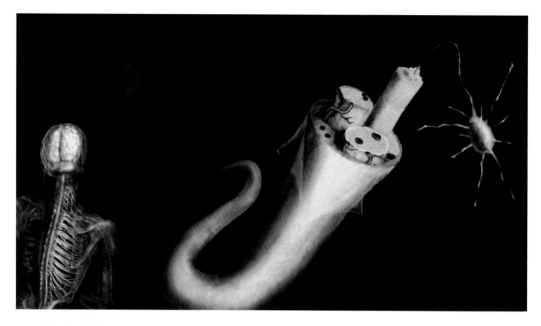

Two kinds of fibers inside nerves carry information from outside the body to the brain or from the brain to other structures in the body.

the spine, from the base of the brain to the hips. This pathway provides the connections between the brain and muscles. When an abnormally formed brain or a brain injury causes disruptions between these connections, problems with movement follow. The infant or child has cerebral palsy.

Billions of cells in the brain send and receive messages to and from all parts of the body. They direct the body to perform movements in response to outside sensory **stimuli,** such as sound, light, space, and temperature. The **cerebral cortex** is the large area of the brain that handles voluntary actions such as thinking, speaking, walking, remembering, and feeling emotions. It also coordinates actions we think about, such as raising a hand in class, reaching for a sandwich at lunchtime, or remembering the movie we saw over the weekend. Generally, the left half of the brain controls functions on the right side of the body, and the right side of the brain controls functions on the left side.

Structures in the **midbrain** are important in voluntary motor movements, as well as in relaying information. At the back of the midbrain is the **cerebellum.** Its Latin name means "little brain," and it is linked to the **motor cortex.** These two structures work together to send information to the muscles, which control movement. The **brain stem,** located at the top of the spinal cord, contains structures that control actions our bodies perform automatically without our having to think about them—breathing, digesting food, and pumping blood, for example.

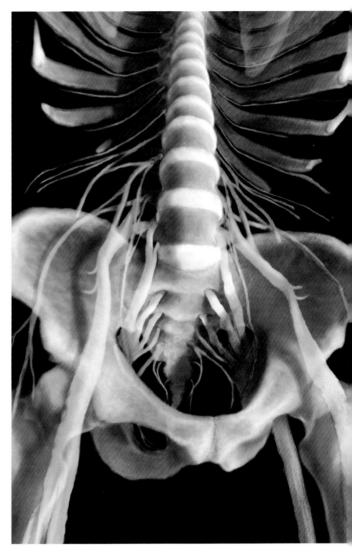

Thirty-one pairs of nerves branch off from the vertebral column to send and receive messages between the brain and muscles.

The cerebellum section of the brain coordinates movement, balance, and posture.

The central nervous system also picks up information from the environment to tell the body what to do automatically. If you are outside on a cold day, your central nervous system will automatically direct blood away from your hands and feet to your heart and organs to protect them from the cold. If a light suddenly goes on in a dark room, the pupils of your eyes automatically adjust to the bright light.

The Peripheral Nervous System

The peripheral nervous system is a network of nerves and white matter connections outside the brain and spinal cord. This system receives information from the spinal cord and sends it to the rest of the body. It is made up of two types of nerves,

sensory and motor nerves. Sensory nerves carry information about senses, such as pain, touch, position, balance, and muscle tension, from the body back to the brain. Motor nerves carry information about movement to the muscles.

Your peripheral nervous system works fast, too, but it involves your **conscious** reactions to outside stimuli. For example if you accidentally pick up a hot pot handle, a message travels from the nerve endings in your skin to nerve cells in your muscles to pull away—fast! If you see a car bearing down on you when you step off the curb, nerve cells in your eyes signal your leg muscles to step back.

Usually these involuntary and voluntary actions happen quickly

Healthy muscles move when the body's nervous systems send instructions on how to move.

and smoothly. However, an injury to the brain, such as the kind that causes cerebral palsy, damages the fast-moving central and peripheral nervous systems. Signals that are supposed to go to and from the motor centers in your nervous systems to the rest of your body may not work the way they do in a healthy brain.

What Goes Wrong

Normally, a healthy brain signals when and how muscles should tighten or relax to maintain **muscle tone.** This is the amount of tightness and looseness your muscles have when you stand, sit, move, or touch something. Some people with cerebral palsy overreact to messages from their brains and have increased muscle tone. Their muscles tighten too quickly and sharply. The muscles may then take a long time returning to a relaxed state or they may remain tight. As a result, the bodies of people with CP may be tense, and they may move stiffly.

Others with cerebral palsy have the opposite problem. They have low muscle tone because their muscles react slowly to messages from the brain. Their muscles are too relaxed. Someone with low muscle tone may have a floppy head, arms, or legs, making it difficult to sit up or walk.

Brain Injury During Pregnancy or Birth

Human brains develop before birth and for many years afterward. Health problems in the pregnant mother can affect brain development. Damage may also result from an injury or accident that happens during the pregnancy, during

Premature babies are at higher risk for cerebral palsy than babies born at the end of a full-term, 36-week pregnancy.

the delivery, or shortly afterward. Risk factors for cerebral palsy include:

- a lack of oxygen before,during, or after birth.
- bleeding in the brain before or after birth.
- multiple births, including twins or triplets.
- diabetes, high blood pressure, or other poor health in the mother.
- severe jaundice (a liver disorder) in newborn babies or low levels of glucose (sugar in the bloodstream).
- an overly long or difficult birth or a premature (too early) birth.

The use of car seats for infants and babies has cut down on the number of head injuries in the past that led to cerebral palsy.

Brain Injuries After Birth

Some injuries to the developing brain take place after birth or in early childhood. These injuries, which may lead to cerebral palsy, include:

- bacterial or viral infections in the brain, such as encephalitis or meningitis.
- a head injury from a fall, an accident, or child abuse.
- rare, inherited diseases that injure the brain.
- injuries during surgery.

TYPES OF CEREBRAL PALSY

Cerebral palsy is usually grouped according to the way the condition affects a person's movement or the way it affects a particular body part.

Spastic Cerebral Palsy

The most common type of CP is **spastic cerebral palsy**. It affects approximately 70 percent of people with cerebral palsy. Spastic cerebral palsy often occurs when an injury damages white matter pathways between the brain and the spinal cord. As a result of this kind of injury, one or more groups of muscles can become tight and stiff most of the time or irregularly. Individuals with spastic CP have problems with their feet as well as with their leg muscles. Their muscles may shorten or tighten around certain joints, especially the ankle, knee, and hip joints. Some individuals with severe symptoms require **orthopedic** (bone) surgery to gain more flexible joint movement. If an individual's mouth muscles are affected, he or she may have problems swallowing, or may drool or have slurred speech.

Ten to twenty percent of people with cerebral palsy develop involuntary movements, such as thrusting the tongue, making twisted facial expressions, spreading fingers involuntarily, and keeping hands, wrists, arms, feet, or legs tightened and bent. Several medical terms describe the types of involuntary movements that can occur in spastic cerebral palsy:

- **Ataxia** describes unsteady, uncoordinated walking or standing, and also indicates trouble with balance.
- **Athetosis** is a description of slow, twisting movements, often of the hands and face.
- **Chorea** means sudden, jerking movements of the head, neck, arms, or legs.
- **Dyskinesia** is a general term for uncontrollable involuntary movements.
- **Dystonia** means repeated twisting postures of the body, arm, leg or face.
- **Rigidity** refers to overly tense muscle tone in any position. This condition seriously limits a person's ability to move.

This girl's walker helps her cope with balance problems due to her cerebral palsy.

Another 10 percent of people with cerebral palsy have what is called a mixed-type condition. They have some difficulties with muscle control, as well as with involuntary movements.

Cerebral Palsy Affecting Individual Body Parts

Doctors, researchers, and other experts in CP, often prefer to use the term that describes the specific part of the body affected by the cerebral palsy. These types include:

- **monoplegia,** which affects only one limb, such as an arm or a leg, on one side of the body.
- **diplegia,** which primarily affects the legs. People with this form of cerebral palsy may stand on their toes or scissor-cross their legs when they try to stand. Their upper bodies often have fewer problems with movement than their lower bodies do.
- **hemiplegia,** which affects one side of the body. A person with this type of CP may not be able to use the affected arm and/or leg very well.
- **quadriplegia,** which affects the whole body, frequently leading to wheelchair use.

"More and more today, professionals shy away from using the term cerebral palsy," says Sue Steindorf, a physical therapist. "It's too broad a description. We would rather say, for example, that a person has diplegia, which means high muscle tone and spasticity of the legs. That is much more meaningful than saying CP."

RELATED PROBLEMS

Sometimes, other conditions besides cerebral palsy appear as a result of injury to the brain or problems in brain development.

Kyle Golizer, who has a form of cerebral palsy that affects his arms, has spoken in public about patients' rights.

Depending on the location of the brain injury, a person with cerebral palsy may also have vision, speech, or hearing problems. Learning disabilities such as attention deficit hyperactivity disorder (ADHD), seizures, or slower-than-average learning skills, may also be a result of brain injury or abnormal brain development. Those who have more severe cases of cerebral palsy are more likely to have problems with eating, breathing, swallowing, speaking, or incontinence (inability to control the flow of body waste).

This boy with cerebral palsy uses a device called a Light Talker to help him with his speech.

3

THE HISTORY OF CEREBRAL PALSY

Although cerebral palsy is not a new medical condition, doctors did not study it closely until the 1800s. The first doctor who wrote about the disorder was an English orthopedic surgeon, named William John Little, who treated conditions related to bones, joints, and muscles. When Dr. Little was a child, he had polio, a disease that affects the muscles and nerves. Because of it, Little had trouble throughout his life controlling movement in his foot. As a surgeon, he wanted to help others with physical disabilities. He established the Royal National Orthopedic Hospital in England.

In the 1840s, Dr. Little studied infants and young children who developed stiff, spastic muscles in their arms and legs. He saw that these children had trouble picking up objects, crawling, walking, and sometimes eating and talking. He described a pattern of muscle problems that appeared to develop in children who had experienced a loss of oxygen during birth or a premature birth. After twenty years of

Cerebral palsy was once called "Little's Disease," after Dr. William John Little, who first described the condition.

studying more than two hundred children with similar difficulties, Dr. Little noted that the children's movements did not improve with age, but also did not grow any worse. He believed that the condition was caused by a brain injury at birth.

In 1889, William Osler, a professor of medicine at the University of Pennsylvania, first used the term *cerebral palsy* to describe the disorder to his students. The word *cerebral* refers to the brain and *palsy* refers to muscle control problems. Like Dr. Little, Dr. Osler believed that cerebral palsy was caused by a complicated birth, loss of oxygen, seizures, or a possible episode of bleeding in the brain before or after birth.

In 1897, the Austrian **neurologist** (a specialist in the brain and nervous system) Sigmund Freud disagreed with the ideas of Drs. Little and Osler. He believed that children who developed cerebral palsy had difficulty with brain development at

Research in the 1980s supported Sigmund Freud's contrary view a century earlier that injuries before birth, as well as afterward, caused cerebral palsy.

some time *before* birth and not necessarily during birth. He based his thinking on the fact that children with cerebral palsy often had other problems relating to brain development, such as seizures or vision and hearing problems, and/or slow mental development. He concluded that a difficult birth was more a symptom of earlier brain damage than a cause of cerebral palsy. Since the 1980s, most medical professionals have agreed with Dr. Freud's explanation. This has led to increased focus on preventing abnormal brain development before birth, which may lead to cerebral palsy. Doctors and researchers are also working to prevent low birth weight and premature birth. These are often associated with cerebral palsy.

Although cerebral palsy is the most common **developmental** disability in the United States, few scientists in the first part of the twentieth century were very interested in studying it. Instead, they concentrated on finding a cure for polio. This paralyzing infection had become widespread by the 1930s. The nation was terrified. But after effective polio vaccines helped to control the disease in the 1950s, researchers were free to spend more time and money studying other diseases. They began to investigate the causes of cerebral palsy and to research possible treatments for the condition.

Beginning in the 1950s, physical therapy became the primary treatment method for children with cerebral palsy.

One of the most important developments in treating cerebral palsy in the 1950s was physical therapy. Dr. Winthrop Phelps, an orthopedic surgeon who founded the Children's Rehabilitation Institute in Baltimore, Maryland, ran the first clinic devoted solely to treating children with cerebral palsy. Doctors researched and carried out new treatment methods.

Pioneers in physical therapy developed new ways to strengthen muscles and teach more efficient motor skills. Occupational therapists, who specialize in guiding hand and arm movements, developed creative ways to teach people with cerebral palsy to write, tie their shoes, cut their food, and pick up small objects. In the 1970s, researchers developed many kinds of **adaptive equipment,** such as braces, casts, and **splints.** This equipment helped support a person's muscles and improve movement. New medications helped patients with seizures and sometimes calmed spastic muscles, as well. Speech and language therapy also became an important part of treatment for people with CP. They helped patients bring together the movements involved in eating, breathing, swallowing, and talking. They also helped people with CP to learn language and other

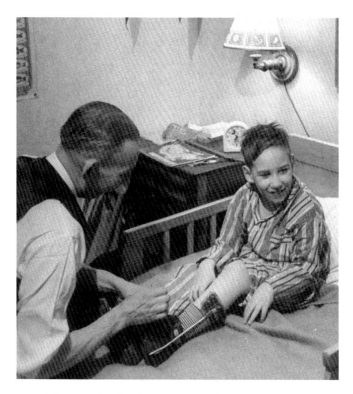

Advances in the development of orthotics, such as leg braces, changed the future for children with cerebral palsy.

ways of communicating, such as using sign language or symbols. One early use of symbols was designed by an engineer named Charles Bliss in the 1970s. Using a set of two thousand symbols, many people with cerebral palsy found Bliss Symbols a useful tool in communicating with others.

An exciting new area of research involves activity-based restoration (ABR). This technique promotes physical and brain recovery in paralyzed people with serious spinal cord injuries. ABR uses a computer to send electrical messages to the injured person's leg muscles to operate a special bicycle. This cycling activity stimulates the development of new brain cells that direct movement. ABR has shown some success in helping people with spinal cord injuries to regain some brain and motor functions. Research using ABR techniques to improve function is beginning for children with cerebral palsy.

EARLY INTERVENTION

Specialists now agree that the earlier therapists begin their work with infants born with cerebral palsy, the greater they will benefit. **Early intervention** programs offer specialized therapy for infants and toddlers from birth to age three. As soon as cerebral palsy is diagnosed, physical, occupational, and speech and language therapists begin treating patients.

Using a variety of exercises, therapists guide their patients through natural and appropriate muscle movements. They show them what a particular motion should feel like. Right from the beginning, these exercises can improve a baby's breathing, eating, and swallowing. The therapy also helps children develop a sense of balance and the ability to hold their bodies in

This student's special desk helps her work independently in a regular classroom.

position. These abilities are automatic in normally developing infants. Infants with cerebral palsy must practice these motions.

Therapists also work with doctors and **rehabilitative specialists** to create effective and more comfortable braces, casts, and **orthotics.** These aids are made of plastic, leather, or high-tech metals. They are formed to fit the patients' bodies, including infants' bodies. The patients wear them to steady their joints and stretch and strengthen their muscles. One therapist says, "Orthotics are like having therapy hands on a child all the time."

LEGAL ACHIEVEMENTS

Some of the most important advances in the care and treatment of people with cerebral palsy have come through laws that help people with disabilities. Up until the mid-1960s, most children with disabilities such as cerebral palsy did not attend public schools. They were kept apart and sent to special schools, institutions, or group homes. Finally, federal, state, and local governments started passing laws that would allow disabled students to attend public schools.

Americans With Disabilities Act

....

"All children, no matter how severe the disability, have a right to a 'free and appropriate' education in the public schools." Part of the Individuals with Disabilities Education Act.

In 1990, the *Americans with Disabilities Act* (ADA) was passed to protect the civil rights of people with disabilities. In both public and private schools, this law helps ensure that students will get the help they need to move around buildings and participate in classroom activities.

In 1965, a federal law called the *Elementary and Secondary Education Act of 1965* (ESEA) was passed. The law was designed to improve public education for all students. An addition to the law included funds to educate children with disabilities in public schools.

Ten years later, in 1975, President Gerald Ford signed a law called *The Education for All Handicapped Children Act* (EHA), which gave more services to disabled children in schools, such as occupational, physical, and speech and language therapy. The EHA has been amended several times since to provide more support for the disabled. The law is now called *Individuals with Disabilities Education Act* (IDEA). Today, IDEA provides funding to educate disabled students in early intervention programs, pre-school programs, kindergarten through high school classes, and beyond. Under IDEA, students with cerebral palsy are entitled to receive therapy, education, and training from birth to age twenty-one.

In recent decades, there has been much progress in medical treatments, as well as in the social acceptance of cerebral palsy. There is so much more to learn about treating the condition, preventing it, and finding new ways for those with cerebral palsy to achieve all that they can.

Famous People with Cerebral Palsy

Christy Brown, author

Chris Fonseca, comedian

Stephen Hopkins, signer of the Declaration of Independence from Rhode Island

Dan Kepplinger, artist

Geri Jewell, actress

Chris Nolan, Irish poet

Thomas Ritter, attorney and founder of United Cerebral Palsy Associations

NEW ADVANCES

While there is no cure for cerebral palsy, modern advances are helping people with cerebral palsy to live with more independence and comfort. In recent years, many new treatments and discoveries have improved the quality of life for people with the disorder. New medications, surgical techniques, brain injury research, therapeutic techniques, alternative therapies, and assistive technology continue to improve the lives of people with cerebral palsy. Doctors and researchers are also investigating ways to help the brain recover from head injuries, which also cause cerebral palsy.

Assistive Technology

In the last two decades, huge strides have been made in multiple technologies. They include a wide range of helpful equipment that helps people with disabilities to participate in everyday activities. Assistive technologies can be items such as easy-to-hold drinking cups, form-fitted car seats, wheelchairs, scooters, or walkers. They also include or electronic devices that help people communicate or use computers such as hearing aids, TTY telephones (telephones that show text messages), switch-operated communication boards, touch screens for computer monitors, special keyboards and computer mice, "talking" calculators, and computer software that recognizes voice commands.

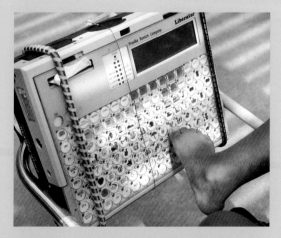

Computers are not just for hands but also for feet, as shown in this liberator device that a seven-year-old is using to communicate.

4

LIVING WITH CEREBRAL PALSY

DIAGNOSIS

Whenever an injury to the developing brain is known or suspected, doctors and parents must watch for early signs that a child may have cerebral palsy. Most children with CP have been diagnosed by age two, unless the condition is very mild.

Infants with cerebral palsy take longer to reach particular developmental stages than infants without CP. They may take longer to roll over, hold up their heads, sit, crawl, walk, or speak. Some infants with cerebral palsy never reach these stages at all. Babies with more severe forms of CP may be unable to eat or swallow.

In addition to such developmental delays, parents and doctors may note a baby's unusual posture and abnormal muscle tone. Some infants with cerebral palsy have **hypotonia,** or low muscle tone, which makes their muscles seem droopy or overly

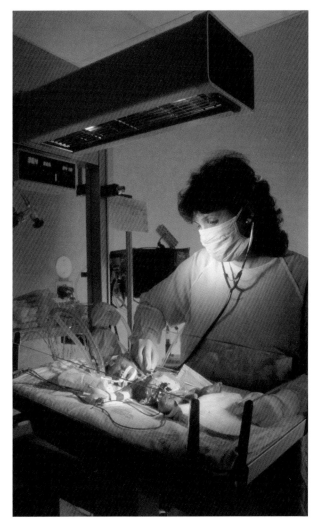

Physical therapy for newborns with cerebral palsy may begin right in the hospital.

relaxed. Others have a condition known as **hypertonia,** or increased muscle tone, which makes the muscles appear very stiff. Some infants with cerebral palsy begin life with hypotonia, and later develop hypertonia. Their muscles are healthy, but the brain is not sending them appropriate messages.

Physicians also test the child's **reflexes,** looking for unusual responses to stimuli. If the child has delayed development and abnormal muscle tone and reflexes, doctors perform tests to rule out other possible diseases.

While there is no single cause and no single test for people diagnosed with cerebral palsy, a brain scan (**magnetic resonance imaging** or **MRI**) can be very helpful in locating a brain abnormality.

This information can then be used to help determine medical treatment, **prognosis** (what may happen in the future), and the rare possibility that other family members are at risk to develop cerebral palsy.

"We cannot tell you if your baby's brain damage is severe enough to mean that she will never walk or talk, or so mild that she might have tight ankle cords and walk with a limp," a doctor told the parents of a baby whose brain was damaged during birth. "Once she matures, we can do some tests, but at this early stage, we do not have any definite answers."

Some of the tests doctors use today to detect cerebral palsy are **CT scans,** MRIs, and **ultrasounds.** Each of these tests shows an image of the brain. A CT scan (Computed Tomography, sometimes called Computer Axial Tomography, or CAT scan) uses computers to take a picture of the brain. An MRI takes an even clearer picture of the brain using strong magnets and radio waves. An ultrasound test, which uses sound waves, is less precise than other tests. But it is also shorter, less expensive, and a more comfortable procedure to undergo. Before the skull bones of an infant's head have grown together, ultrasounds can pass through and reveal scars or other damaged areas in the brain.

Cerebral palsy appears at different levels of intensity: mild, moderate, or profound (severe). People with mild cerebral palsy need little assistance and can usually care for their own daily needs. People with moderate cerebral palsy need help with their daily needs and require orthotics, braces, walkers, or wheelchairs. People with severe or profound cerebral palsy need help with most daily activities.

Symptoms vary with each individual with CP. Those who have other medical problems, such as seizures, visual or mental impairments, or hearing loss, need additional care and treatment. Regardless of whether a child has cerebral palsy that is mild, moderate, or severe, parents and caregivers must act as soon as possible to work with a treatment team.

After a diagnosis of cerebral palsy, a child responds best under the care of a team of doctors, therapists, and specialists.

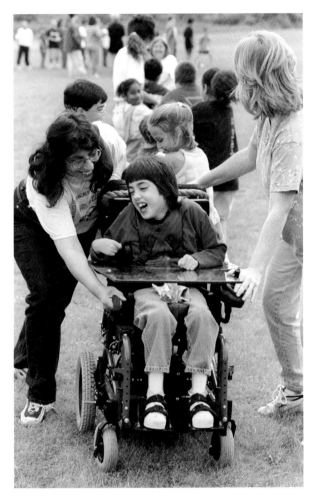

Lightweight wheelchairs, with many features, have made it possible for children with CP to participate as fully as possible in school activities with the general school population.

Members of the treatment team may include a neurologist, an orthopedist, a physiatrist (a doctor who specializes in physical therapy and rehabilitation), a developmental pediatrician (a doctor who treats children with growth and motor problems), speech and language pathologists, and physical and occupational therapists. Other specialists should be involved if there are additional medical problems, such as vision or hearing difficulties. Together, the team and the child's family focus on developing skills and improving muscle function. Ideally, these efforts should begin at infancy and last a lifetime.

Frequent physical therapy can strengthen the range of motion in many children with cerebral palsy.

TREATMENTS FOR CEREBRAL PALSY

Speech and language therapists are responsible for helping their patients control mouth and jaw muscles. For infants, these therapists guide and stimulate the muscles that are used in sucking, swallowing, and eating. In older children, speech and language therapists help children to speak more clearly. They also teach alternative communication skills such as sign language and the use of symbols, computer equipment that speaks, or communication boards. These boards fit on a lap or attach to a wheelchair. Some have alphabet blocks or easy-to-push buttons that are programmed to say certain words and phrases. Besides "Hello," "Thank you," and "Goodbye," the boards can be personalized to help a person say "I would like some apple juice please" or "I want to go swimming."

Physical therapy develops large motor skills. These are any

This girl's wheelchair, which helps her to get around, is outfitted with a computer she uses for communication with others.

movements involving the large muscles of the body, such as the legs, arms, and abdomen. Physical therapists work to increase the **range of motion** and muscle strength. Range of motion is the ability of joints to go through full movements. Physical therapists use exercises and equipment such as therapy balls, stair steps, and bicycles to help with balance and posture. "When kids are young, I focus on their needs one on one, but when kids get older, I like to do therapy with groups, because it is fun," explains one elementary school physical therapist. "For instance, if I want the kids to work on the range of motion of their knees, we have a tea party on the floor, and we squat!"

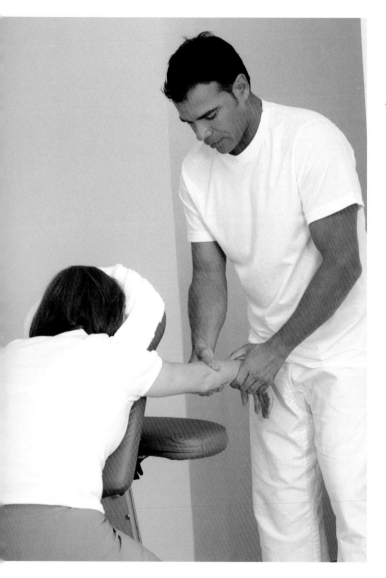

Physical therapy helps to tone muscles that cerebral palsy has damaged.

Assistive Aids and Technologies

To prevent muscles from becoming stiff or weak, physical therapists work with orthopedists to develop individualized orthotics to strengthen and support muscles and joints. Orthotics can help a person to become more independent. Once a person grows used to wearing orthotics, he or she is often much more comfortable *with* them than without them.

Physical therapists also teach people how to use canes, walkers, and wheelchairs. Walkers are lightweight metal structures with four legs and a curved handle. Some have wheels. Some have seats. Many people who use wheeled walkers keep the walker behind them and slightly lean back against it for support. Some people who use wheelchairs have manual chairs that they operate by pushing a bar connected to the the wheel. Others use motorized wheelchairs that are

A back walker keeps this girl strong and tall.

battery powered and can be controlled by using switches, a joystick, or voice-activated commands. Choosing the right wheelchair is a major decision. There are many questions to ask when buying a wheelchair. Will it be used outside or only inside? Will it be taken on a bus or in a car frequently? Will it be used all the time, every day, or only occasionally? One sixth-grader said that her parents made all those decisions, but she was able to make the most important one—"What color?" She chose bright purple.

Occupational therapists are very creative in finding ways to help make everyday tasks easier for their patients. They supply or make special straps, handles, or grips for spoons, forks, knives, cups, pens, pencils, and markers. Children will often practice tying, buttoning, or snapping snaps using special boards or different strategies. Therapists also match students' abilities to assistive technologies, such as large-button computer keyboards, touch screens for computer monitors, and software programs that make typing easier. As one occupational therapist says, "I look at what a kid *can* do and look at what he or she *wants* to do, and then I find a way of putting it all together!"

Medications

Physicians can prescribe muscle-relaxing medications to ease the effects of cerebral palsy. These medications control muscle

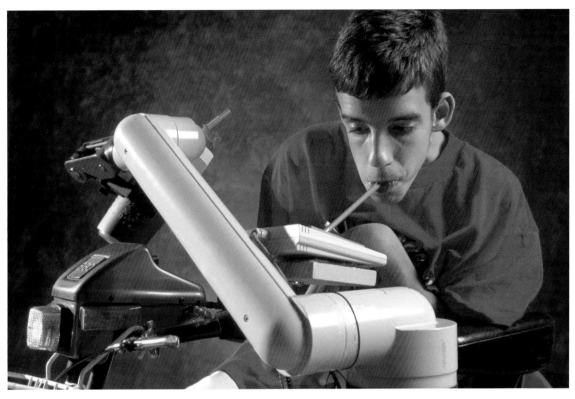

This young teen with cerebral palsy uses a pencil in his mouth to operate his computer.

contractions and spasms. Some of these medications may improve hand use, speech, or **mobility.** Unfortunately, some medications cause unpleasant **side effects** such as slurred speech, drowsiness, and digestive problems. So patients and their families need to work with doctors to find the dosages that provide the best balance between benefits and side effects.

Sometimes, doctors will inject a medication such as Botox directly into a stiff and shortened muscle to relax it. During this treatment, doctors and therapists can work on strengthening and stretching the muscle by using therapy, as well as casts, and other orthotics.

Another alternative treatment is the use of a specialized pump, placed in the abdomen. The pump sends medication directly to the spinal cord. This treatment reduces overly tight muscle tone.

For people who have severe cerebral palsy, a doctor may suggest surgery to help correct shortened or tightened muscles.

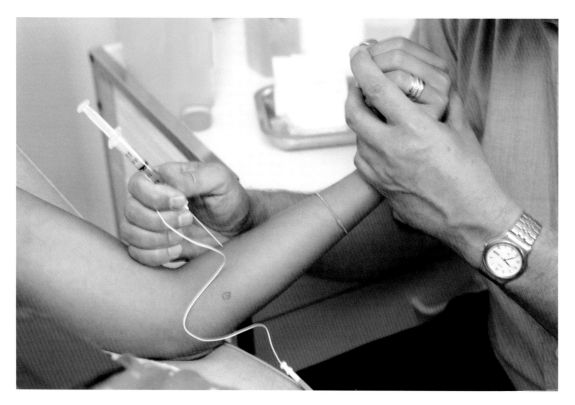

Injections of a drug called Botox can improve the movement of overly tight muscles associated with cerebral palsy.

Using a test called **gait analysis,** doctors can note how a person walks and which muscles and tendons are causing problems. Doctors can then target the shortened and contracted muscles or tendons and lengthen them surgically.

Surgeons are using new techniques in the hope of correcting faulty signals sent by the brain to the nerves. One operation for helping severe muscle contractions is called "selective dorsal rhizotomy." In this type of procedure, overactive nerves that cause extreme leg contractions are cut, thereby reducing spasticity. Surgery may not be the answer for everyone. But for some, it makes an important difference in comfort and independence.

DAILY LIVING

Cerebral palsy cannot be cured. However, treatment and therapy are the keys to living as full, happy, and independent a life as possible. Various therapies are a lifelong part of the lives of many people with cerebral palsy. Therapy helps a baby with CP to eat, sit, and crawl. For toddlers, therapy helps a child walk, climb, or balance. A child can learn to stack blocks, throw a ball, or color with a crayon. As the years go by, therapy helps students to write or type on a keyboard. Orthotics and mechanical aids, such as wheelchairs and walkers, help people better explore and experience the world around them.

Like anyone growing up and having new experiences, people with cerebral palsy sometimes face fear, disappointment, and

Advances in voice-activated computers have made it possible for many patients to use computers even without the use of their arms and hands.

loneliness. For a student, it is hard not to feel singled out and different if he or she is the only person in the classroom in a wheelchair. Orthotics, walkers, and communication boards all seem strange and a little frightening to someone who has never seen them before. People with cerebral palsy and their friends, siblings, and teachers should understand that when others stare or look away, they may be naturally curious. Educating others about CP helps others learn what it is and what strengths and limitations someone with the condition has.

"It's important to be matter-of-fact about cerebral palsy," advises one school therapist.

To carry this out in one third-grade classroom, a teacher noted that a student with cerebral palsy seemed to be struggling with feeling accepted. So the teacher decided to talk about people's individual differences. She started a conversation about herself and the things that she felt made her different from others. Then she asked the students to speak up. A few responded, but many did not. The room grew a little quiet and a little uncomfortable. Some of the students looked over at the boy with cerebral palsy who wore braces on his legs and used crutches to walk. In turn, the boy looked around the room and raised his hand. The teacher called on him. He said, "I am different from everyone else in this room. I actually *like* broccoli!" Of course, the whole class laughed. Everyone realized that despite any differences, people share many of the same feelings and ideas.

Many enjoyable everyday activities can provide the same physical benefits as therapy, along with the fun of social connections. Many people with cerebral palsy swim, cycle, bowl, work out at the gym, and dance. They participate in regular sports and adaptive sports, such as wheelchair basketball. Some become involved in Special Olympics competitions. Most communities have public pools, and scholarships for sports participation. A growing number have therapeutic horseback-riding programs.

Sibshops

The **siblings,** or brothers and sisters, of people with developmental disabilities, have special needs, too. They often experience situations and events that are quite different from those of their friends at school. For example, people ask uncomfortable questions, or even make fun of the disabled person. Also, many siblings of people with disabilities feel that their parents expect more from them than they should. Others simply wish that their disabled brother or sister could be more of a companion. Feeling singled out in these ways can be lonely. Nationwide, the Sibshops program helps the siblings, or "sibs," of people with disabilities cope, learn, laugh, play, and talk things over.

Sibshops are usually held on Saturday afternoons and are generally open to children ages eight to thirteen. Only the non-disabled sibling attends. This encourages the siblings to share feelings they may feel reluctant to express at home.

Meetings begin with a get-acquainted activity, such as designing a face nametag. The rest of the day is filled with activities such as cooking, games, arts and crafts, sharing stories, and making friends. Sometimes guests visit. One such guest at a recent Sibshop was an artist with cerebral palsy who taught the siblings how to paint while holding paintbrushes in their mouths. The group admired the artist's skill and saw how difficult it was.

During a typical Sibshop, there are several opportunities for "sibs" to chat about the ups and downs of living with a disabled sibling. After attending a few Sibshops, "sibs" realize that they are not alone. They discover that they *and* their disabled brother or sister are amazing, and that they have new friends with whom to share common feelings and ideas.

You can find a Sibshop by going to this Web site: http://www.thearc.org/siblingsupport/sibshops-directory.shtml

Therapeutic horseback riding can help a person with cerebral palsy develop balance and confidence.

At home, family members should encourage and support stretching programs. "As children with CP grow older," explains physical therapist Sue Steindorf, "they must face the fact that they will always have spasticity, **contractures,** and stiffness. They need to take responsibility for their own bodies by creating a lifestyle and following a stretching program, with habits that will make them healthy and strong for life. It's just like brushing our teeth. We all take time to brush every day.

That's what people with CP have to do—take the time to stretch and exercise every day."

Mak, a boy who has diplegia, is a terrific example of someone who makes healthy choices to fit his needs and interests. When he was younger, Mak, who wears braces on his legs, played T-ball with the other first graders. He loved baseball, collected cards, and knew all his favorite players' statistics. But as he grew older, the Little League teams grew more competitive, and Mak stopped playing. But he did not stop going to games. Every afternoon in the spring, Mak walked to the ball field to watch the Little Leaguers practice or play. At practices, he would help out by collecting baseballs lying in the outfield, or by giving the batters pointers about the other team's pitchers. At games, he sometimes would sit in the announcer's booth and help call the games, or he would assist with keeping the scorebook. Whether he helped out or not, he watched the games with a fan's interest. After a game, people in the stands always offered to give Mak a ride home. But even when it rained, he would politely say no. "Walking back home is my workout," he would say. Mak's dedication to his sport and to his own condition shows that people with cerebral palsy, their families, and their caregivers, should seek treatments and activities suited to them. This effort will enable them to live their lives as independently and fully as possible.

The Sporting Life

Two international programs recognized by the International Olympic Committee invite disabled athletes to participate in many competitive sports.

Special Olympics
The motto of the Special Olympics is *"Let me win. But if I cannot win, let me be brave in the attempt."* Athletes compete, but the true emphasis is on achieving physical fitness, meeting personal goals, and participating with others interested in the same sport. Special Olympics is open to anyone with a disability, particularly anyone with a developmental disability. It was founded in 1968 by family members of President John F. Kennedy, whose sister was disabled.

The Paralympics
The Paralympic Games began in 1960 as a way for highly athletic people with disabilities to compete in sports. Summer and winter games are held at the same time and in the same host city as the Olympic Games. Paralympic athletes take the same pledge as Olympic athletes. Six general disability groups compete in the Paralympics program, one of which is reserved for athletes with cerebral palsy. Most of the competitions are the same as those held in the Olympic Games. However, there are a few additional competitive events, such as wheelchair tennis and wheelchair rugby.

Wheelchair basketball is a great schoolyard sport, as well as an official Special Olympic sport.

GLOSSARY

adaptive equipment—The devices that offer special support to a
person with physical disability.

assistive technology—The equipment used to maintain or
improve skills for people with disabilities.

ataxia—Unsteady, uncoordinated walking and/or standing.

athetosis—Twisting movements of the hands and face.

brain stem—The base of the brain located just above the spinal
cord.

central nervous system—The tissues in the brain and spinal
cord that control activities in the body.

cerebellum—The part of the brain that controls motor activity.

cerebral cortex—The major part of the brain located at the front
of the skull.

cerebral palsy—A group of developmental disorders that affects
a child's movements.

chorea—A form of cerebral palsy marked by sudden, jerking
movements of the head, neck, arms, or legs.

conscious—Aware and responsive to surroundings.

contractures—Conditions in which muscles become fixed in a
rigid, abnormal position.

Computerized axial tomography (CAT scan)—A computerized
imagine technique that takes pictures of the brain.

developmental—The state of growing and development.

diplegia—A cerebral palsy condition that affects both legs.

disability—The inability to do something because of a problem with the body or mind.

dyskinesia—Uncontrollable, involuntary movements.

dystonia—Slow, repeated twisting of the body, arm, or leg.

early intervention—The kinds of newborn and infant programs, which offer therapy to help lessen the effects of disabilities.

fetus—An unborn human.

gait analysis—A technique that uses cameras and computer analysis to measure a person's walking pattern.

hemiplegia—A form of cerebral palsy that affects one side of the body.

hypertonia—Increased muscle tone, or stiffness.

hypotonia—Decreased muscle tone, or relaxed, floppy muscles.

Magnetic resonance imaging (MRI)—An imaging technique that uses radio waves, magnetic fields, and computer analysis to create a picture of body tissues and structures.

midbrain—The middle section of the three parts of the brain.

mobility—The ability to move.

monoplegia—A cerebral palsy condition that affects only one limb.

motor cortex—A part of the brain that sends messages to nerve cells involved in movement.

muscle tone—The level of tightness or relaxation of muscles.

nerves—The bundles of fibers that send information from one part of the body to another.

nervous system—The pathways made up of nerve cells that send signals from one part of the body to the other.

neurologist—A doctor who studies the central nervous system and the treatment of disorders of the nerves and brain.

neurons—A special type of cell that sends messages to and from the brain.

occupational therapists—The professionals trained to treat fine motor movements.

orthopedic—Relating to a branch of medicine that deals with bones.

orthotics—Lightweight plastic, leather, or metal devices that support joints and gently stretch muscles.

para-educators—Classroom assistants who help students with learning disabilities.

peripheral nervous system—The nerve tissues outside the spinal cord and brain.

physical therapists—Professionals trained to treat motor movements performed by the large muscles, such as those in the arms, legs, and abdomen.

prognosis—The likely outcome of a physical problem.

quadriplegia—A form of cerebral palsy that affects the whole body.

range of motion—The amount of movement performed by a joint.

reflexes—The movements that the body makes automatically in response to stimuli such as light and temperature.

rehabilitative specialists—The health professionals who help people with brain injuries to regain brain and motor functions.

resource room—A separate classroom that is available to a special education teacher who teaches students with disabilities.

rigidity—Overly tense muscle tone in any position.

seizures—Sudden, abnormal electrical discharges in the brain that cause temporary, uncontrollable movements and loss of consciousness.

sensory—Relating to the senses, such as sight, sound, smell, taste, and touch.

siblings—A person's brothers and/or sisters.

side effects—The unwanted results of using a particular medication.

spastic cerebral palsy—The type of cerebral palsy associated with tight, stiff muscles.

special education—The school instruction programs that are designed to meet the individual needs of disabled students.

spinal cord—The bundle of neurons running inside the spine, which carries messages between the brain and the body.

splints—Devices made of molded plastic and straps used to stretch muscles or to hold a limb in place.

stimuli—Something that brings about a reaction or response.

ultrasound—A medical device that bounces sound waves off of tissues and structures in the body to create an image.

vertebral column—The bony covering of the spinal cord.

white matter connections—The pathways made up of nerve bundles that carry messages to and from the brain.

FIND OUT MORE

Organizations

American Academy for Cerebral Palsy and Developmental Medicine
555 East Wells Street, Suite 1100
Milwaukee, WI 53202
414-918-3014
www.aacpdm.org

This is a scientific society concerned with cerebral palsy education, treatment, and research. There are many reports and fact sheets available online.

National Easter Seals Society
230 West Monroe Street Suite 1800
Chicago, IL   60606-4802
800-221-6827
www.easterseals.com

This organization is dedicated to helping people with disabilities learn about new research, therapies, surgery, and medications. The Society also publishes many information booklets and sponsors Special Needs summer camps around the country.

National Information Center for Children and Youth with Disabilities (NICHCY)

P.O. Box 1492
Washington, D.C. 20013
800-695-0285
www.nichcy.org

This organization provides information on education and special services for people with disabilities. Look on the Web site for State Sheets Resource that provide useful local programs and support.

National Institutes of Health National Institute of Neurological Disorders and Stroke (NINDS)

Building 31, Room 8A06
Bethesda, MD 20892
301- 496-5924
www.ninds.nih.gove/disorders/disorder_index.htm#C

This is the Web site of the U.S. government agency that studies brain and nervous system disorders and provides education to the public. Follow links to the Disorders section *Cerebral Palsy* then the link to *Hope through Research* pages. You can order pamphlets and read about new developments in cerebral palsy research.

United Cerebral Palsy (UCP)
1600 L Street NW Suite 700
Washington, DC 20036
800-872-5827
www.ucp.org

UCP is a national organization for people with CP and their families. Contact local chapters for information and support in your area. The Web site has many articles and fact sheets to download.

Books

Carter, Alden R. *Stretching Ourselves: Kids with Cerebral Palsy* Morton Grove, IL: Albert Whitman & Co., 2000

Gilman, Laura Anne, *Coping with Cerebral Palsy*. New York: Rosen Publishing Group, 2001.

Sachar, Louis. *Small Steps.* New York: Delacorte Press, 2006.

Web Sites

International Center for Disability Resources on the Internet
(Follow the Cerebral Palsy link on the home page)
www.icdri.org

International Paralympic Committee (IPC)
www.paralympic.org

Kids Health–Cerebral Palsy
www.kidshealth.org/kid/health_problems/brain/
    cerebral_palsy.html

National Center on Accessible Information Technology in
Education (AccessIT)
www.washington.edu/accessit

Special Olympics
www.specialolympics.org

INDEX

ABOUT THE AUTHOR

Ruth Bjorklund lives on Bainbridge Island, a ferry ride away from Seattle, Washington, with her husband and two children. In researching this book, she formed a strong appreciation for the courage shown by young people with cerebral palsy and for the caring concern of their parents, friends, teachers, and health care providers.